O Bethlehem

The story of Jesus' birth
Micah 5:2–5; Luke 2:1–20; and
Matthew 2:1–11 for children

Written by Joan Petersen Tietz
Illustrated by Dave Hill

CONCORDIA PUBLISHING HOUSE • SAINT LOUIS

O Bethlehem, O Ephrathah,
You're just a little town.
Tremendous plans by God Himself—
His love, it has no bounds!

O Bethlehem, O David's town:
The birthplace of a king.
For out of David's promised line,
God's Son to us He brings.

A Shepherd King was to be born
To guard and keep His sheep,
The strength and majesty of God
To bring eternal peace.

O Bethlehem, you chosen town,
The time was drawing near.
God's only Son was to be born
To Joseph, Mary dear.

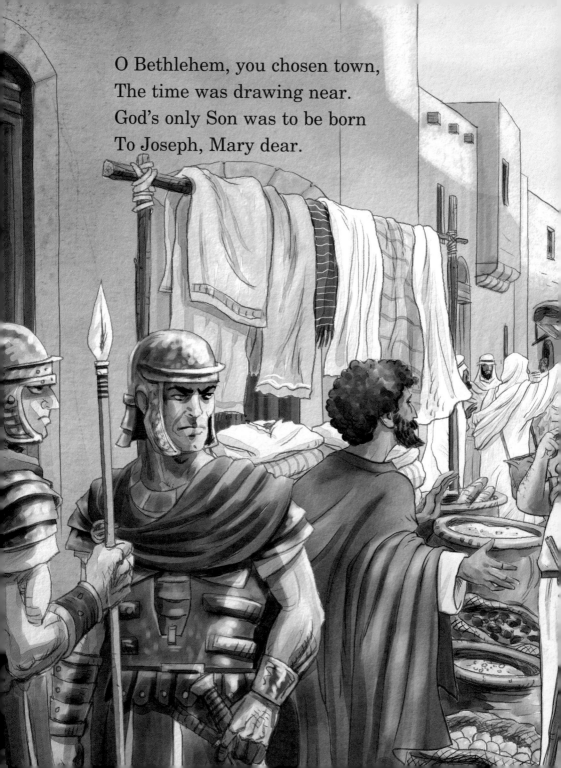

Census required that tax be paid;
Joseph and Mary came.
O Bethlehem! You welcomed them
To streets of little fame.

The inns were full, you crowded town,
O little Bethlehem!
A lowly stable stall was all
The room you had for them.

No palace grand in Bethlehem
To greet the Prince of Peace—
He had a manger for His bed,
Warmed by lamb's soft fleece.

O Bethlehem, in humble hills,
The shepherds watched with care
And kept their flocks with sleepy eyes
When angels did appear!

The glory of the Lord shone down
And filled the men with fright.
"Fear not," proclaimed the heavenly host,
"The Christ is born this night!"

To Bethlehem the shepherds ran,
Their Lord in Mary's care.
Amazed and honored, they bowed down
And praised their Lord most fair.

O joyful town of Bethlehem,
The shepherds were so blessed!
The Word made flesh was laid right there,
Poor shepherds—honored guests!

O Bethlehem, you city small,
Your streets are dark and dim,
But God has placed a wondrous star
To light the way to Him.

O distant town of Bethlehem,
The Wise Men from afar
Were sent a promised sign from God:
A new and glorious star!

O silent town of Bethlehem,
The wise men bowed and knelt,
Gave praises to the baby boy.
God's presence now they felt.

O Bethlehem, O Ephrathah:
The least of Judah's clans.
But God chose only you to be
Fulfillment of His plan!

For God has special plans for us.
He's given us His Son!
Messiah, Savior, Shepherd King,
Heaven for us He won!

Dear Parents,

The familiar carol "O Little Town of Bethlehem" contrasts the dark and light—the darkness of night with the light of the stars, the darkness of sin with the light of Christ. It may be because of this carol that we think of Bethlehem as a quiet little town, but when Joseph and Mary journeyed there, the town was anything but. It would have been teeming with people, crowded to capacity, and quite noisy! And as the prophesied birthplace of the Messiah (Micah 5:2), it would have had the attention of religious leaders of the day, even as the people there had been living out their day-to-day lives for hundreds of years without incident. Still, Bethlehem was insignificant compared to Jerusalem, a few miles away.

Talk to your children about God's chosen birthplace for His Son and how God often uses the small and unlikely to do His will. Tell your child that like Bethlehem, God has unique plans for him or her. Just as God chose that little town for a special purpose, He chooses us for His purposes too (see Ephesians 2:8–10).

Give this book additional depth by incorporating activities when you read it. Draw the town of Bethlehem together. Read the verses from Micah. Talk with your child about God's promises in the Bible. Remind him or her that Christmas is all about the gift of God's one and only Son—the holy Child of Bethlehem— to save us from our sins.

To Him be the glory! Alleluia!

The Author